**GEO**

10104

D1120004

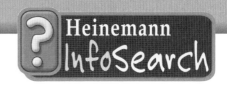

# SCIENCE ANSWERS

# Microlife

## FROM AMOEBAS TO VIRUSES

Heinemann Library
Chicago, Illinois

**Anna Claybourne**

Design: Richard Parker and Celia Floyd
Illustrations: Art Construction
Picture Research: Rebecca Sodergren
  and Pete Morris
Originated by Dot Gradations Ltd.
Printed in China by WKT
  Company Limited

08 07 06 05 04
10 9 8 7 6 5 4 3 2 1

**Library of Congress Cataloging-in-Publication Data**
Claybourne, Anna.
  Microlife : from amoebas to viruses /
Anna Claybourne.
    v. cm. -- (Science answers)
  Includes bibliographical references and
index.
  Contents: What are microorganisms? --
What kinds of microorganisms are there? --
Where are microorganisms found? -- How
do microorganisms live? -- How do
microorganisms help us? -- How do
microorganisms harm us? -- People who
found the answers -- Amazing facts.
  ISBN 1-4034-4768-3 -- ISBN 1-4034-5514-
7 (pbk.)
  1. Microbiology--Juvenile literature. [1.
Microbiology. 2. Microorganisms.] I. Title.
II. Series.
  QR57.C537 2004
  579--dc22
                              2003025665

**Acknowledgments**
The author and publishers are grateful to
the following for permission to reproduce
copyright material:

p.4 Kwangshin Kim/Science Photo Library;
p.5 Dr. Tony Brain/Science Photo Library;
pp.6, 27, 28 Science Photo Library; p.7
Pascal Goetgheluck/Science Photo Library;
pp.8, 14 David Scharf/Science Photo
Library; p.9 Charles Daguet/Institut
Pasteur/ Petit Format/Science Photo
Library; pp.10, 25 Eye of Science/Science
Photo Library; p.11 Martin F.
Chillmaid/Science Photo Library; p.12
National Cancer Institute/Science Photo
Library; p.13 NASA/Science Photo Library;
pp.15, 17, 23 Tudor Photography/Harcourt
Education Ltd.; pp.16, 20 Andrew
Syred/Science Photo Library; p.18 A. B.
Dowsett/Science Photo Library; p.21 St.
Mary's Hospital Medical School/Science
Photo Library; p.22 David Munns/Science
Photo Library; p.24 Getty Images; p.26
Doug Martin/Science Photo Library; p.29
Gilette Corporation/SPL.

Cover photograph reproduced with
permission of Juergen Bergen/Max Planck
Institute/Science Photo Library.

Some words are shown in
bold, **like this.** You can find
out what they mean by
looking in the glossary.

# Contents

## About the experiments and demonstrations

This book contains some boxes called Science Answers. Each one describes an experiment or demonstration that you can try yourself. There are some simple safety rules to follow when doing an experiment:

- Ask an adult to help with any cutting that uses a sharp knife.
- After any experiment involving microorganisms, wrap up all the disposable materials in a plastic bag and throw them away.
- Thoroughly wash your hands and any containers you have used.

## Materials you will use

Most of the experiments and demonstrations in this book can be done with objects that you can find in your own home and food you can buy cheaply from a store. You will also need a pencil and paper to record your results.

# What Is Microlife?

Microlife is a general name given to small living things called microorganisms. The word *micro* means "very small," and **organism** means "a living thing."

Microorganisms are much smaller than other small organisms such as ants and flies. In fact, microorganisms are too small to see without a microscope. Although normally you cannot see them, there are millions of microorganisms all around you. They live in water, soil, air, food, and even inside your body.

### Important microorganisms

Microorganisms are incredibly important, not just for humans, but for the whole planet. They feed on other living things that have died, helping to **recycle chemicals** back into the soil. They help the human body work. People also use different kinds of microorganisms to make chemicals, medicines, and foods such as bread, cheese, and yogurt.

At the same time, some microorganisms can create problems. They can cause diseases that harm people, animals, and crops. They can make food go bad, rot people's teeth, and make water supplies, kitchens, and hospitals unsafe.

## Sometimes dangerous?

The microorganism in this picture is a type of **bacteria** called *Escherichia coli.* It is shown here through a microscope. *E. coli* lives in human **intestines** and it is usually harmless. However, some types of *E. coli* can give you a bad stomachache if you swallow them.

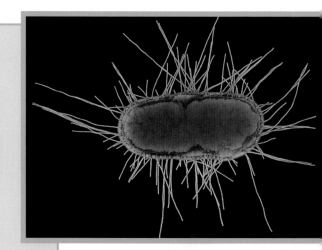

## The size of microorganisms

Microorganisms are all small, but they still come in a range of different sizes. A typical **bacterium** such as *Escherichia coli* measures about one **micron** across. A micron is one thousandth of a millimeter. About 250,000 *E. coli* bacteria could fit on the period at the end of this sentence.

However, a single bacterium is big compared to a **virus,** the smallest kind of microorganism. A typical virus is only one thousandth the size of an *E. coli* bacterium. You could fit 250 million of them on the period at the end of this sentence.

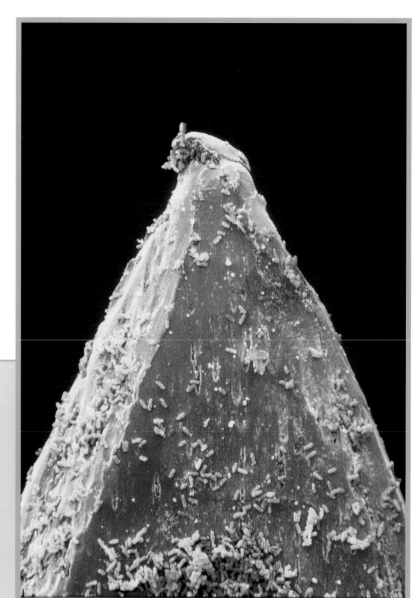

## Magnified microorganisms

In this magnified photograph you can see rod-shaped bacteria (colored orange here) on the tip of a syringe needle. They appear hundreds of times bigger than they are in real life.

## The discovery of microorganisms

People have only known about microorganisms for around 350 years. This is because they can be seen only with microscopes. The first microscopes were invented around 1600. By the 1650s microscopes became powerful enough to show larger microorganisms such as **bacteria.**

One of the first people to see microorganisms was the Dutchman Anton van Leeuwenhoek (1632–1723). In a scientific experiment in 1683, he took some **plaque** from the teeth of two old men who had never cleaned their teeth. Under a microscope, van Leeuwenhoek saw bacteria swimming around. He called them *animalcules.* Over the next 200 years, microscopes got better and better. More microorganisms were discovered and named.

## Scientific discoveries

In the 19th century, scientists such as Joseph Lister, shown here at his microscope, realized that some microorganisms could **infect** wounds and cause diseases.

## More names for microorganisms

Like other living things, most **species** of microorganisms have been given scientific names. For example, the bacteria that causes a deadly disease called anthrax is named *Bacillus anthracis*, or *B. anthracis* for short. Scientific names are in Latin and are written in italics. People also use the general name *germs* to talk about microorganisms that cause diseases.

## Looking at microorganisms

The first microscopes used glass lenses like those in magnifying glasses to make objects look bigger. Some microscopes still work this way, including the light microscopes often used in classrooms. Today the most powerful modern microscopes are huge, expensive **scanning electron microscopes.** They work by firing **electrons** at a microscopic object. When the electrons bounce back, they form a pattern. A computer turns this pattern into a picture and displays it on a computer screen. Most of the pictures of microorganisms in this book were taken using a scanning electron microscope. The pictures are black and white at first. Color is added later to make the pictures clearer.

# What Kinds of Microorganisms Are There?

Many microorganisms are single-**celled,** which means that they are made up of just one cell. Cells are the building blocks of all living things. The human body, for example, is made up of millions of cells. Each cell is too small to be seen on its own. But each cell contains what is necessary for life.

Microorganisms can be divided into several main groups. **Bacteria** are single-celled microorganisms that do not have **nuclei. Viruses** are the smallest microorganisms. They are not made up of cells. **Algae** are single-celled **organisms** that make their own food like plants. **Protozoa** are single-celled organisms that move around like animals. **Fungi** and molds are single-celled microorganisms related to mushrooms.

## What is a bacterium?

A bacterium is a very common kind of microorganism. Bacteria have only one cell and are often round or sausage-shaped. Some kinds of bacteria can cause diseases, but most of them are harmless or even useful. They are found in many places. This image shows bacteria on a kitchen sponge.

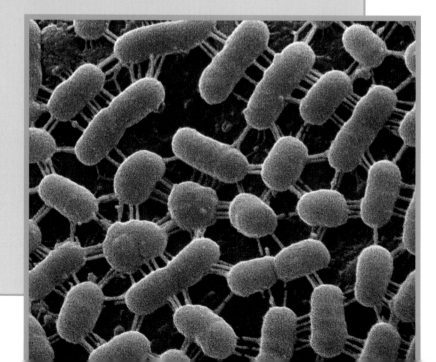

Some kinds of very small multicelled organisms are also called microorganisms because they can only be seen with a microscope. One example of a multicelled microorganism is the nematode worm.

## Are viruses alive?

Viruses, which are the smallest microorganisms, are unusual because they are not made of cells. A virus is much smaller than a cell. Some scientists say viruses are not really living things at all because they do not eat or breathe and cannot **reproduce** on their own. Instead, a virus works by attacking a cell and using the cell to make copies of itself. Viruses are so small that they can reproduce inside bacteria and other cells. The flu and the common cold are examples of diseases caused by viruses. This series of pictures shows a virus invading a human cell.

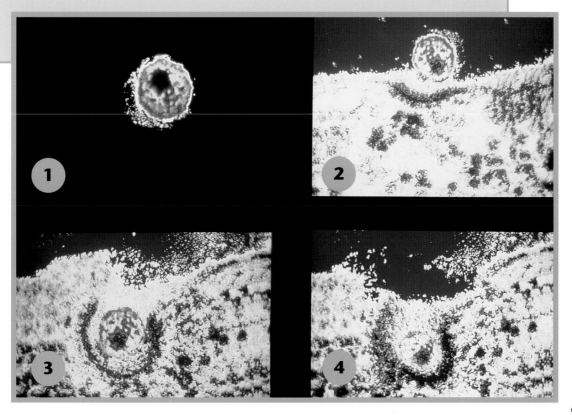

## More microorganisms

Some microorganisms live like single-**celled** plants while others move around like animals. **Algae** are like small plants. They float in water or grow on damp surfaces. Like plants, algae need sunlight to survive. Although one alga is too small to see except through a microscope, you can sometimes see a greenish tinge in a pond or fish tank where millions of algae are living. Just like plants, algae give off **oxygen** as they feed.

**Fungi** grow on rotting fruit and vegetables, or on living things. For example, athlete's foot, which grows on people's feet, is a type of fungi. So is yeast, which people use to make bread rise. Molds include things like the black mold that grows in damp bathrooms and the jellylike slime mold that sometimes grows on grass in wet areas. You can see these things because you are looking at billions of microorganisms growing together in a group. Each individual microorganism would be too small to see by itself.

## Single-celled animals

**Protozoa** are like very small animals. They are usually made up of just one cell. Protozoa move around by stretching and shrinking themselves, or by waving tiny hairs or finger shapes. Some protozoa cause diseases such as **malaria.** Here, malaria protozoa called *Plasmodium falciparum* (yellow) burst out of human red blood cells.

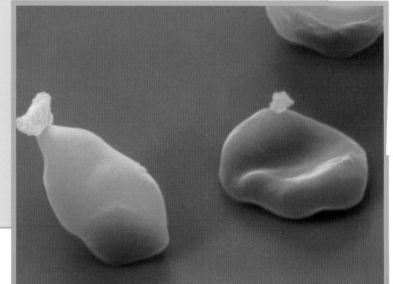

## Living together

Many kinds of microorganisms, such as algae, **bacteria,** yeast, and slime molds, live together in big groups called **colonies.** The colony grows into a bigger and bigger mass as the microorganisms **reproduce.** Although they cannot talk to each other like people do, scientists think the microorganisms in a colony may send each other messages using **chemicals.**

## A yeast colony

This block of baker's yeast is made up of millions of single-celled **organisms.** Scientists say that yeast cells can communicate with each other using chemical signals.

# Where Are Microorganisms Found?

Microorganisms are found in most places. Soil is full of **bacteria, algae,** worms, and other microscopic **organisms.** Other bacteria, **viruses,** and **protozoa** live in or on larger living things such as plants, animals, and people. In a typical house, there are bacteria in food, on damp cloths, on door handles, on telephones, and on anything else that people touch. **Fungi** can live on rotten food, around bathtubs and toilets, and in damp corners.

### At home in the heat

Some amazing bacteria, called **thermophilic** bacteria, like to live in boiling hot water. They are found around **hydrothermal vents,** where hot springs bubble up from cracks in the seafloor. They feed on **minerals** in the water.

## Dangerous water

Water usually contains some microorganisms. Algae and protozoa float in oceans, rivers, lakes, and ponds. The drinking water that comes out of our taps also contains a few harmless bacteria. But in some parts of the world, drinking water may contain microorganisms that cause serious diseases such as **bilharzia.** Bilharzia is caused by the bilharzia flatworm shown here. If people bathe in or drink water with this flatworm, it can make them very sick or even kill them.

## How do microorganisms move from place to place?

Microorganisms need to move around to find food and places to live, but only a few of them can move by themselves. Protozoa and worms can swim or crawl along, but bacteria, algae, fungi, and viruses usually just float around. They are moved from place to place by wind, water or by other living things. For example, a bacterium in the air could land on a leaf, which could then be eaten by a cow. The bacterium could then grow and **reproduce** in the cow's body. Some of the bacteria might leave the cow's body in its dung and land in the soil, and so on. Some viruses, such as the common cold virus, can be spread through the air from one person to another by a cough or sneeze.

## Are there microorganisms in space?

Some scientists think there is evidence that a kind of small, bacterialike microorganism once lived on the planet Mars. If they are right, this will be the first life ever discovered on another planet.
The tubelike structure shown in blue was found on a meteorite that came from Mars.

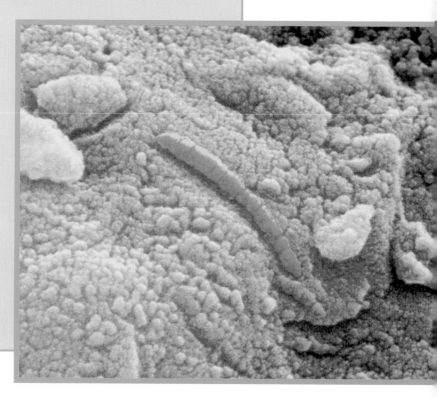

## Where are most microorganisms?

Most microorganisms find it easiest to survive in warm, damp places where there is plenty of food and water. There is not much microlife in the sands of a hot, dry desert, or in the ice at the top of a mountain. However, there are huge numbers of microorganisms in soft, damp soil. One handful of soil can contain up to six billion **bacteria.** That is almost as many human beings as there are on Earth.

The same thing is true in people's homes. The biggest numbers of microorganisms are found in warm, damp places such as a pot of soup that has been left out on a warm day. In these conditions, any bacteria in the soup will be able to keep feeding and **reproducing** until there are millions and millions of them. The human body is a perfect home for microorganisms, too. **Fungi** can live on your skin. **Viruses** can invade your body and give you diseases. The large **intestine** is home to billions of bacteria that help with **digestion.**

### At home in the soil

The *Bacillus* bacteria shown here live in the soil. Warm, moist soil provides all the food and warmth these microorganisms require. They feed on dead and **decaying organic matter.**

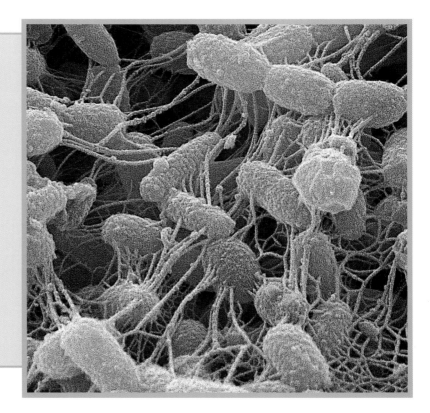

# EXPERIMENT: Does milk spoil faster in or out of the fridge?

## HYPOTHESIS
Milk will spoil faster if it is kept warm.

## EQUIPMENT
A carton of fresh milk, two clean glasses, a refrigerator, a pen, paper

## STEPS
1. Pour some milk into each glass. Put one glass of milk in the refrigerator and the other in a warm place such as a sunny windowsill.
2. On a piece of paper, write down how the milk in each glass looks and smells. Then, at the same time every day examine the glasses again and write down how the milk looks and smells. Continue the experiment for up to three days. Then throw the milk away.
3. Write down what you saw.

## CONCLUSION
The milk that is kept warm changes much faster than the milk that is kept cold. The warm milk starts to smell bad and look lumpy. This is because the bacteria in it can reproduce much faster in warm temperatures. The milk in the fridge will take much longer to spoil because bacteria reproduce much more slowly in the cold.

# How Do Microorganisms Live?

Like other living things, most microorganisms need food and water to stay alive. Many also need **oxygen,** although a few kinds of **bacteria** do not need oxygen to survive. Many microorganisms need sunlight, too. When they have everything they need, microorganisms can grow and **reproduce.**

## Microorganism food

Just like humans, most microorganisms feed on **organic matter.** For example, the bacteria that live on people's teeth eat sugar from the food that passes through people's mouths. Mold growing on bread feeds on the bread. Yeast feeds on the sugary **chemicals** found in some foods. Bacteria such as *Streptococcus pyogenes* eat living flesh. **Algae** and some types of bacteria are like plants. They turn sunlight into food. Some microorganisms eat other microorganisms.

## Eating without mouths

Most microorganisms do not have mouths. They eat by soaking up food through their skin or, like this amoeba (shown in green), by wrapping themselves around their **prey.**

## Why are viruses different?

Unlike other microorganisms, **viruses** do not eat, breathe, or grow. Instead, they simply **replicate,** or copy themselves. They do this using materials from the **cells** of other living things.

## ACTIVITY: Make a mold garden

Molds can grow on most foods at room temperature. Some foods will get moldy more quickly than others.

### EQUIPMENT
A large, clear glass or plastic container or jar with a lid that can be thrown away; different kinds of food such as fruit, bread, cake, cheese, and potato chips; paper; pen

### STEPS
1. Wash out the container.
2. Take each piece of food and dip it in water.
3. Put all the food in the container and put the lid on.
4. Leave the container in a well lit place at room temperature. Check the container daily and write down what you see.
5. As the food starts to get moldy, describe and draw what you see.

### EXPLANATION
Different types of mold grow on different foods. Some foods take longer than others to get moldy. This is partly because some packaged foods such as potato chips contain preservatives. These are chemicals that make it harder for mold to grow.

### Reproduction

Although microorganisms do not have babies in the same way that humans do, they do **reproduce** and make copies of themselves. **Protozoa** often do this by simply splitting in two. Some types of **fungi** release **spores,** which are like small seeds. The spores float away in the air, and they may grow into new fungi wherever they land. Microscopic worms lay eggs that grow into new worms.

### How do bacteria reproduce?

Most **bacteria** reproduce by dividing. To make new bacteria, a single-**celled** bacterium grows bigger and bigger. It makes a copy of its **genes,** which are the instructions inside it that make it work. Then the bacterium separates into two new cells, each with its own copy of the genes. The new bacteria are exact copies of the parent bacterium. They are called daughter cells.

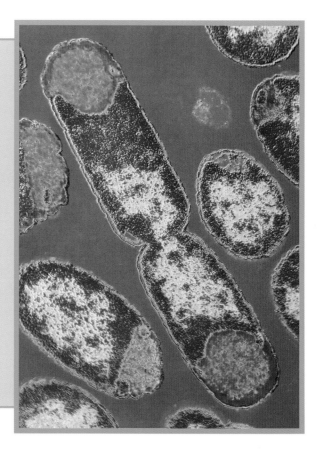

## Microlife multiplication

Microorganisms such as bacteria, which reproduce by splitting in two, can multiply very fast. Each new bacterium divides into two more, and each of those divides into two more, and so on, causing a bacteria population explosion. Bacteria such as these *Escherichia coli* can divide every twenty minutes. At this rate, as long as there is enough food and moisture, one *E. coli* bacterium can turn into more than a million bacteria in just seven hours.

# How do viruses replicate?

**Viruses** can only **replicate** by invading a cell, which could be a bacterium or an animal's body cell. A virus contains a set of instructions for making copies of itself. The virus replicates by forcing a cell to follow these instructions. Here is how it works:

**1** The virus approaches a cell.

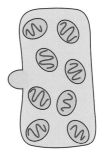

**4** New viruses are formed within the cell.

**2** The virus sticks to the cell surface and forces its genes into the cell.

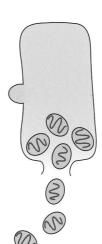

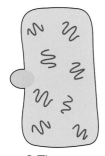

**3** The genes multiply inside the cell.

**5** The cell bursts and the new viruses are released.

# How Do Microorganisms Help Humans?

Some people think of microorganisms as bad or dirty, but many kinds of microorganisms are essential to life on Earth. The most important job microorganisms do is make things rot. When a plant or animal dies and **decays,** it is actually being eaten by **bacteria,** worms, **fungi,** or other microorganisms. They break down the **chemicals** in things that have died and **recycle** them back into the soil. These chemicals then help plants grow, making new food for other living things. If microorganisms did not do this, dead plants and animals would never decay. They would just pile up on Earth's surface!

## Bacteria inside your body

Many of the billions of bacteria living inside your body are good for you. For example, *Bifidobacteria* in your large **intestine** make **vitamins** that help your body. *Lactobacillus bulgaricus,* visible here as long, pink strands in yogurt, guard your intestines against other bacteria that can cause diseases.

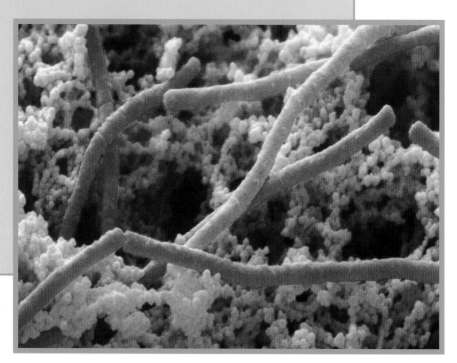

## Microorganisms help animals that people eat

Microorganisms are also important for animals that people eat, such as cows. The foods that cows eat, such as grasses, are very hard to digest. A cow's stomach is full of bacteria and **protozoa** that can break down tough grasses and turn them into chemicals. The cow's body uses these chemicals to grow and make milk.

## How did Fleming discover antibiotics?

In 1928 British scientist Alexander Fleming experimented with a kind of mold that was growing on an unwashed dish in his lab. The mold was able to kill disease-causing bacteria. He realized that the mold, called *Penicillium*, was releasing chemicals that were destroying the bacteria. These chemicals, which were later found to be made by various kinds of microorganisms, are now known as **antibiotics.** They are often used to treat illnesses and **infections** caused by bacteria.

## What do people use microorganisms for?

Microorganisms are used in factories and homes to make foods such as bread, cheese, and yogurt. Over thousands of years, humans have discovered that certain microorganisms give foods pleasant tastes and textures. For example, when yeast feeds on sugar it gives off bubbles of **carbon dioxide** gas. These bubbles give bread a soft, spongy texture as it bakes.

There are many other products besides food that contain microorganisms or **chemicals** made by microorganisms. For example, some types of detergents contain chemicals called **enzymes** that help get rid of stains on clothes. These enzymes are made by kinds of **bacteria** that are found naturally in soil. Microorganisms are also used to make medicines, kill insect pests, and process **sewage** and other waste.

### Using microorganisms with milk

Bacteria are used to turn milk into yogurt. Cheeses such as Roquefort (seen here) and blue cheese contain greenish blue molds. These molds give cheese a tangy taste.

# DEMONSTRATION: Feeding yeast

Yeast feeds on sugar and makes bubbles of gas as a waste product.

## EQUIPMENT
Two packets of dried yeast, two small bowls, a teaspoon, a cup, sugar, warm water, paper, pencil

## STEPS
1. Put a cup of warm (not hot) water and the contents of a packet of yeast into each bowl and stir.
2. Add a teaspoon of sugar to one bowl and stir.
3. Put both bowls in a warm place such as a sunny windowsill.
4. After ten or twenty minutes, write down what has happened.
5. When you are finished, throw away the contents of the bowls.

## EXPLANATION
The yeast in the bowl with sugar will produce bubbles as it feeds on the sugar. The bubbles appear as a foam on top of the water. When the yeast has no sugar to feed on, it makes hardly any bubbles.

# How Do Microorganisms Harm Humans?

While some microorganisms are useful, some bother humans, and others can even be deadly. Microorganisms can cause diseases, make food spoil, and destroy crops. Microorganisms that cause diseases include many types of **bacteria** that can cause sore throats, **tuberculosis,** and **meningitis. Viruses** cause colds and the flu, as well as **AIDS** and many other serious diseases. **Protozoa** cause **malaria** and **bilharzia,** which often make people ill in warm climates. Bacteria and **fungi** can get into wounds and cause blood poisoning or gangrene, which makes flesh rot away.

## How do germs cause diseases?

Germs often cause diseases because they make **chemicals** that are bad for your body. Also, the way they **reproduce** and feed can damage your **cells.** Germs **infect** humans because our bodies provide them with the warmth, water, and food they need to survive. The illnesses they cause are just a side effect. The person shown here is suffering from a common cold caused by a virus.

## Rotting food

It is natural for meat, vegetables, and other foods to **decay** over time. But this causes a problem when people want to store food or transport it long distances. If food spoils, that means it contains a lot of bacteria. Spoiled food can taste bad or even make you ill.

## What do bacteria do to teeth?

Teeth make a good home for bacteria such as *Streptococcus mutans.* There are a lot of nooks and crannies for them to hide in, and there is food constantly passing by for them to eat. Unfortunately for humans, when these bacteria feed on sugar they produce an acid that eats away at teeth, making them decay. Brushing your teeth to clean away the bacteria (shown here as a yellow coating on a tooth surface) helps to prevent decay.

### Fighting germs

Your body has an **immune system** that fights off most germs. But sometimes your immune system needs help. Scientists have discovered many medicines and treatments that kill disease germs or keep them under control. We can control the spread of germs by cleaning kitchens, bathrooms, food factories, and hospitals with germ-killing **chemicals** such as bleach. Keeping food in the refrigerator or freezer and thoroughly cooking food makes it harder for germs to **reproduce.** Washing your hands after you go to the bathroom helps control germs, too.

## Creating a barrier

One of the best ways to keep germs out of the places we do not want them is by using the barrier method. A barrier is created between a possible source of germs and the thing people want to keep free from germs. This is why nurses and doctors wear gloves, gowns, and masks during operations. It is also why people who prepare and serve food wear gloves and caps.

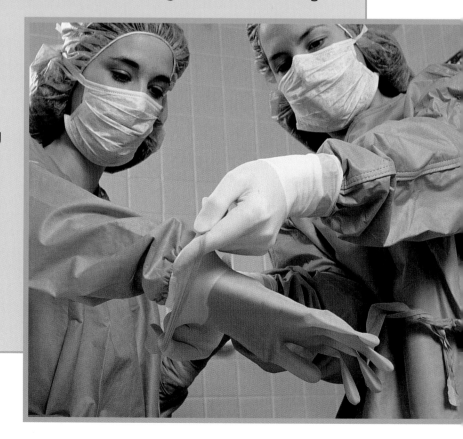

## Some microorganisms harm plants and animals

Just like humans, plants and animals can catch diseases and **infections** caused by microorganisms. In fact, many microorganisms only affect a particular **species** of plant or animal. For example, some cat diseases are caused by different **viruses** that only affect cats. Microorganisms can harm wildlife, too. Hundreds of gorillas in Africa have died after catching a deadly virus called Ebola.

## Trouble for farmers

Microorganisms can be a big problem for farmers. **Fungi** and viruses can damage crop plants like potatoes and coffee. The picture below shows a lettuce damaged by a fungus called *Sclerotinia.* Farm animals such as cows and sheep can get diseases caused by microorganisms that can be fatal. When germs kill farm crops or animals, it affects

people's food supply and can even cause a **famine.** This happened in Ireland in the 1840s, when a potato fungus spread across the country. Millions of people did not have enough food, and up to a million people died of hunger.

# People Who Found the Answers

## Ignatz Semmelweiss (1818–1865)

Semmelweiss worked as a doctor in a hospital in Vienna, Austria in the 1840s. He ran two **maternity wards.** One ward was staffed by **midwives,** and one was staffed by doctors who also worked in other wards. He noticed that in the doctors' ward, mothers were much more likely to catch **infections** and die in childbirth. He realized that the doctors must be spreading germs to the maternity ward from other parts of the hospital. By making the doctors wash their hands after seeing each patient and change their clothes after operations, he greatly reduced the rate of infection. The doctors were so angry about the new rules that Semmelweiss was fired. But his methods were soon adopted in other hospitals and are still important today.

## Louis Pasteur (1822–1895)

Before the 19th century, many people thought that microorganisms grew by themselves out of nonliving matter such as mud or water. In the 1860s, Louis Pasteur, a French scientist, proved that this was not true. He showed that microorganisms could spread from one place to another in the air, and that they could **reproduce,** cause diseases, and spoil food. His work led to major

advances in medicine and food preparation. Pasteurized milk, for example, is named after Louis Pasteur. It is milk that has been heated to kill any **bacteria** in it.

# Amazing Facts

- Experts think there may be as many as ten million different **species** of microorganisms. However, not all species have been discovered and named. There are probably more microorganism species than species of all other living things put together.

- The **protozoan** that causes **malaria** is one of the most dangerous living things ever—at least for humans. More than one million people die from malaria every year.

- Diseases caused by microorganisms kill about seventeen million people around the world every year.

- Microorganisms were the first living things on Earth. Scientists say microorganisms first developed in mud or water about 3.5 billion years ago.

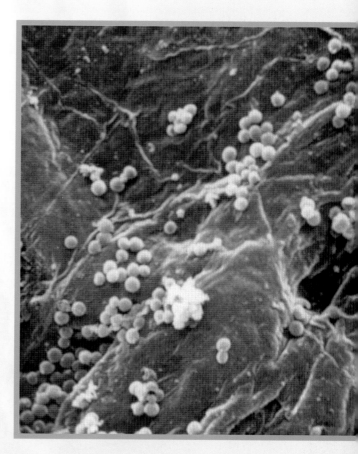

- One square inch (6.5 square centimeters) of your skin has around 60 million microorganisms living on it. This picture of bacteria on skin was taken by a **scanning electron microscope.**

# Glossary

**AIDS** (Acquired Immune Deficiency Syndrome) disease that damages the body's immune system

**alga** (more than one are algae) single-celled organism that makes its own food like a plant

**antibiotic** chemical that fights bacteria. Antibiotics can be made by some kinds of molds.

**bacterium** (more than one are bacteria) common single-celled organism with no nucleus

**bilharzia** disease carried by a flatworm that lives in water

**carbon dioxide** gas found in small amounts in air. Plants use it for photosynthesis and animals breathe it out.

**cell** building block of living things that can only be seen with a microscope. Most plants and animals are made up of millions of cells.

**chemical** basic substance that things are made of

**colony** group of organisms that live together

**decay** break down or rot

**digest** break down food into nutrients that an organism can use

**electron** tiny particle. Electrons are part of the atoms that all substances are made up of.

**enzyme** protein made by living things that helps a chemical reaction to occur

**famine** widespread lack of food

**fungus** (more than one are fungi) type of living thing that is not an animal or a plant. Fungi include mushrooms, molds, yeasts, and toadstools.

**gene** code carried in a cell that determines how it grows

**hydrothermal vent** crack in the seafloor that releases hot water from inside Earth

**infect** enter and start to reproduce inside an organism

**immune system** set of organs and cells in your body that work together to fight germs

**intestine** long, coiled tube that is part of the digestive system

**malaria**   disease caused by a protozoan that is spread from one person to another by mosquitoes

**maternity ward**   area of a hospital where women give birth

**meningitis**   disease that affects the layers surrounding the brain

**micron**   thousandth of a millimeter, or 0.00004 inches

**midwife**   person who helps women give birth

**mineral**   chemical building block of rocks

**nucleus** (more than one are nuclei)   part of a cell that helps control the life processes within the cell

**organic matter**   group of substances that are alive or were once alive

**organism**   living thing

**oxygen**   gas in the air which many living things need in order to survive

**plaque**   thin coating of pieces of food and bacteria on teeth

**prey**   animal that is caught and eaten by another animal

**protozoan** (more than one are protozoa)   small single-celled organism that moves around

**recycle**   change something old into a new form so it can be used again

**replicate**   make exact copies

**reproduce**   make young

**scanning electron microscope**   very powerful microscope

**sewage**   human waste from toilets and sinks

**species**   group of organisms that have similar characteristics

**spore**   small, seedlike object that some fungi and molds use to reproduce

**tuberculosis**   disease that affects the lungs and bones

**thermophilic**   able to survive at high temperatures

**virus**   microorganism that survives by invading the cells of living things

**vitamin**   useful chemical

# ▶• More Books to Read

Gareth Stevens Publishing Staff. *Viruses*. Milwaukee: Gareth
   Stevens, 2003.

Pascoe, Elaine. *Single-Celled Organisms*. New York: Rosen
   Publishing, 2003.

Spengler, Kremena. *Louis Pasteur*. Minnetonka, Minn.: Capstone
   Press, 2003.

# Index